Copyright 2017 By

James Barry Edwards

ISBN 978-0-9994261-0-4

Published By Humor House

Everything Trump Will Do For America

Everything Trump Will Do For America

Everything Trump Will Do For America

Everything Trump Will Do For America

Everything Trump Will Do For America

Everything Trump Will Do For America

Everything Trump Will Do For America

Everything Trump Will Do For America

Everything Trump Will Do For America

Everything Trump Will Do For America

Everything Trump Will Do For America

Everything Trump Will Do For America

Everything Trump Will Do For America